BEST CHINA SKY

Carol Rumens was born in 1944 in London. A former poetry editor of *Quarto* and *The Literary Review*, she has held several writing fellowships, most recently at Queen's University, Belfast. She has won several prizes for her poetry, including the Alice Hunt Bartlett Award, the Cholmondeley Award and the Prudence Farmer Award, and all her Bloodaxe collections have been Poetry Book Society Recommendations or Special Commendations. She is a freelance writer, and lives in Belfast.

Carol Rumens has published nine books of poetry: *A Strange Girl in Bright Colours* (Quartet, 1973); *Unplayed Music* (1981) and *Star Whisper* (1983) from Secker; *Direct Dialling* (1985), *Selected Poems* (1987) and *From Berlin to Heaven* (1989) from Chatto; and *The Greening of the Snow Beach* (1988), *Thinking of Skins: New & Selected Poems* (1993) and *Best China Sky* (1995) from Bloodaxe. She has also written plays, short stories and a novel, *Plato Park* (1987), and has edited two anthologies, *Making for the Open* (Chatto, 1985) and *New Women Poets* (Bloodaxe Books, 1990).

Her first play, *Nearly Siberia*, was premièred by Pascal Theatre Company in 1989. She is an occasional translator of Russian poetry, and has a group of translations in Irina Ratushinskaya's collection *Pencil Letter* (Bloodaxe Books, 1988). *The Greening of the Snow Beach* includes some of her translations of Blok and Mandelstam, while *Best China Sky* includes translations of Yevgeny Rein, Boris Slutsky and Bella Akhmadulina. She is the editor of Elizabeth Bartlett's *Two Women Dancing: New & Selected Poems* (Bloodaxe Books, 1995).

CAROL RUMENS

Best China Sky

BLOODAXE BOOKS

Copyright © Carol Rumens 1995

ISBN: 1 85224 337 6

First published 1995 by
Bloodaxe Books Ltd,
P.O. Box 1SN,
Newcastle upon Tyne NE99 1SN.

Bloodaxe Books Ltd acknowledges
the financial assistance of Northern Arts.

Cover printing by J. Thomson Colour Printers Ltd, Glasgow.

Printed in Great Britain by
Cromwell Press Ltd, Broughton Gifford, Melksham, Wiltshire.

Acknowledgements

Acknowledgements are due to the editors of the following publications in which some of these poems first appeared: *As Girls Could Boast* (Oscars Press, 1994), *Fortnight, Irish Review, Irish Studies Review, Poetry Now, The Poetry of Perestroika* (Iron Press, 1991), *Poetry Wales, The Rialto, Soundings, The Times Literary Supplement,* and *Ulster Newsletter*; and to BBC Radio Ulster, which broadcast some of the poems.

I would like to thank Yurij Drobyshev for his help in the Russian translations. We dedicate these translations to the memory of Piotr Mononen (*d.* Siege of Leningrad, 1942).

Contents

LEARNING TO BE MORTAL

HOME FIRES

Railway Lullaby

Little train-lover, there's pink sky in your speckled window.
There'll be a bridge, a bay, a child's sea, rippling:
All the details exactly as you'd have crayoned them.
I promise, I promise, to take you nowhere but home.
Lean your brow to the glass, I'll shake very gently.
The dragon's in his box, his breath pure puffs of snow.
Five decades later, my gas-dim stations
Will glow for you again behind your drifting eyes,
Go out, one by one, and be gone for ever.

Distances

When she falls backwards and meets the fire and the rain,
Last of her generation in this absurdly continent family,
Who will remember her, make a note of her overwhelming virtues,
And colourful evasions: who will truthfully describe
The face that always remained a stubborn child's,
Outstaring us with hardiness, impudence, fear:
Who will follow that stare to the father:
Who will stand at the grave and tell him she was hurt:
Who will show the mother and sister what they stole:
Who will ask the young man, disappointed and disappointing,
For one of those Valentine poems she smiled at and soon mislaid
(The ever-blue handwriting knotted with shyest self-declaration):
Who'll untangle the whiteness and free all the numerous shapes
       of her lips?

They will say, those greatest of aunts, those most-removed cousins
Whose names she almost remembered, that it's not up to them
Since she leaves a child: this is the child's business.

Don't look at me. I'm innocent. I'm not the one
To speak of the dead. I can't even speak to the living.

A Short Life with Gratispool

Another Soldier (1945)

The Baby's only ever snapped
In Daddy's arms, maybe to bring it home
How like as two peas their heads –
Though Daddy usually hides
Most of his in one of them forage-caps
Which, thankfully, this nipper won't have to wear –
Though Old Jeremiah, snooping in the pram,
Puts Mummy's back up, whining, 'What you got there?
Another soldier?'

Workers' Playtime (1948)

There's no room for any more,
Mrs Moore. No more twinkles
In Daddy's eye. We try. We're on the Housing List.
The LCC Man wrinkles
His nose and says our drainage is A1,
And tons of space for another tot. But what
If it's a boy? And even if it's not,
Four in a room's a bit much.
So, hard luck, my old Dutch.
Soon as we can we'll follow the van.
Meanwhile, on with the show.
Turn the pages, stay as sweet as you are.
Mummy's gathering moonbeams home in a jar,
Daddy's singing Oh, Mein Papa,
And occasionally getting pissed,
And the Victory Baby's growing quick, quick, slow
Into an Only One. Ain't we got fun?

Scarlet Ribbons (1957)

'By twelve years old, everything is accomplished':
And now you can see
That, despite puff-sleeves and plaits like paint-brushes,
She's almost made up her mind to run away.

Though the snaps are posed and dead,
She's always almost in motion, half up a tree
Or straddling a bike. (You can't see,
Of course, but bike and ribbons are red.)

Soon as Dad's boxed the Brownie in, she's gone,
Pedalling up a speed
That makes a mockery of holding on.

No hands, no hands, watch me
Never never never going home for tea –
The loose ribbon flying its trickle of blood.

What Can I Say About My Grandfather?

You were born in March, good month for a blusterer.
Sixty years on, you lead me up the garden-path.
I am accused of beheading chrysanthemums.
Your rage convinces me, I'll sign the confession.

You turn dull cloth into suits in a cedar-wood shed.
I thump my ball at the side when the treadle's silent.
You've lost your famous account with the local convent.
You call the nuns *sharks* or *schneiders*. You call me *Saletch*, and *Missie*.

And you're in a rage because your baby son died.
And you're in a rage that you fathered 'an old woman's child.'
You say: 'Leave them on the window-sill, it's kinder.
You don't know when you're well-off, Missie. You're *all right*.'

You give me a fiver for passing the Scholarship.
But my craze for classical music's 'all put on'.
Your fingers swell. It's rheumatism. It's cancer.
The room where I played the piano becomes a sick-room.

Fierce light leaks under the door on the day of your funeral.
I stare in the hall-mirror, between the permed heads
Of the shop chrysanths, to study my Christmas sweater.
The sweater's hairy. Tight. I'm too old for Christmas.

I still hate remembering how you'd looked in bed.
You seemed so meek and thin, so bloody grateful.
Mum said: 'Pop was a first-class tailor and cutter.'
She'd never learned to sew. I've never believed in 'all right'.

Home Fires

Hope was the tenderness
That healed the heart
When fingertip kisses first
Began to melt
The place without a name,
She would tease herself, as the flame
Teased yesterday's news –
Battle-cries of the *Express*,
Twisted in gawky love-knots
By her sweet-faced corporal,
Down on his knees, and missing
His train to demonstrate
A further useful art.
Thus beautifully immersed,
She would forget how most
Scripts seemed to end:
The groans, the gunshots,
The dying turmoil
On the cold side of the bed,
Where, unable to move,
She'd know she was badly wounded,
And this, for all its grace,
Had not been the making of love,
Still less, the coming of peace.

1950

(from the Russian of Yevgeny Rein)

The cable-car rises, a red-hot blaze, to the Sanatorium Frunze
(Named after Ordjonokidze), sends a mirror of light to the coast-road.
There's plenty of choice in the shops here – from eighths of litres
    to halves.
On your left, the Diplomat's Rest House. Journalists go straight ahead.
We're not far from Sochi. I'm seeing all this for the very first time.
Wearing my jersey-knit trunks with the sky-blue *Dynamo* band,
I lounge in the shade of a beach-umbrella, or hurl myself through
    the frontline
Of the quarrelsome breakers pitched steadily over the sand
By some Lord of the median term, some Black Sea spirit,
Looking out of the depths at the twentieth-century's backside.
There's womanly flesh in abundance – milk, terra-cotta, chocolate,
But the tastiest colour by far is that of a dumpling, deep-fried.
Everything's fine and appalling, and something is almost made clear.
Around sunset, a sense of foreboding creeps out of the Caucasus.
Closing your eyes, you're alarmed when dull, reddish pimples
    appear
In the lids like an eczema-rash, or some kind of horrible pox.
Koba's sun is still high; over Moscow and Ritsa, its zenith.
This same mountain eagle sees all, his attention is double-bright.
Whatever you know, protect. Keep your head down. Cherish
Yourself like your sight.

Curriculum Poetica

Fountains are mostly light:
    A lough or tarn
Is the bland, incomparable
    Centrefold
Where breathless mountains yearn:
    Waterfalls dramatise
Earth's slightest *Oh*.
    But a stream, star-crossed,
Learns from the grass in its eyes
    Its profile's low.
Good enough to undazzle
    To the valley's level,
Still it's begrudged:
    Poor tinkling harper,
Pebble-prospector, tapster
    To witch and woad-man;
Hanger-out in the sticks,
    Grateful to be lodged
In cul-de-sacs blessed by
    Local voluminous slops.
How can it shine without sky?
    Without fire, foam over,
Lusty as loving-cups
    At the gods' table?
Mud is its pulse if mud
    Its course and kiddle,
Its art, a lament
    In curious hieroglyphs
Some clever-clogs will propose
    Is just the usual
Nattering on about
    Old roots, lost nymphs,
    And, any way, in prose.

England

It became so old,
It turned into a baby.
Teach it language, world.

From the Anglo-Saxon

Visit me again, one of these evenings.
Bring the gift of your small self, wisely hooded in wool,
The cold-blush winging your face, your eyes all flight.
Let my shadow befriend your slowly settling shyness.
Come without being called, without first calling.
I'll have the coal bright, the bottle cold, in no time.
Tap at my door, my window, I'll welcome you always –
I, who rise helplessly when the hollowest fingers
Flutter and flap at the letterbox-flap, let it go.

The Con

There's a knack but it's a bit of a con, like.
Don't ask me how I first twigged.
I prob'ly just want to kid meself
I always knew in me bones, like you did.

It wouldn't work now, that's for sure.
You'd say: you're kidding, mum, you're a fucking
Lezzie, you are,
If I told you how, when me tit, like,
Poked you in the mush, you'd do a double-take

And, quick as a flash, start sucking.
Even when I'd just got you fed,
You was still the same little clinger.
You come on like a limpet,
Even when I was just messing,
Just tickling your mush wiv me finger.

The Purr

When the boy knew he would never be listened to,
He fell asleep. This photograph confirms it:
Sleep in the boy's hand, reaching absent-hearted
To smooth the equable forehead of *Morsilka:*
Sleep in the purr we hear from her tabby frown,
Her barrelled rump, the powder-puffs of her haunches:
Sleep in the stern, near-masculine little profile
That denies itself a study, though the father
Shouts *Keep still,* and the glass eye glares: that denies
It could ever meet desire in a woman's look.
Morsilka, the boy's slyly parted lips
Are saying in cat-talk: *Morr, Morr, Morsilka.*

Dormancy's always attractive in a man –
Ask the rise-and-shine brigade of his admirers.
When he was 25, they'd have cut their names
In his skin to see the colour of his eyes –
Too late, by a hundred years!
He slept and slept, heavy as the Ukraine
In Europe's gut, as vodka on the liver,
Woke to father a child or two, fell away
To deeper sleep, his electrician's hands
Curling into their knowledgeable darkness.
Now when I pause, the last straggler, coldly
Equable in the beam of his sleeping vision,
I deem it a privilege not to be roughly parted,
And thrown on like a favourite dressing-gown,
But wear my own hand, guiltlessly and lightly,
And murmur self-talk: *Morr, Morr, Morsilka.*

Because my foam will never trouble him,
I leave it on his lips, free of charge.
Because it speaks my favourite language, silence,
I make sleep-love to his carved and studious back.
His rest and my retreat are perfect partners
Like boy and cat. Or, like a woman, found
By the only woman, when the long notes drawn
At length from one another's sleeping fur
Call back the dawn before we fell asleep

To bear the breaking day, that utterly clear
Wakefulness. *Morsilka*, our smiles say
Might be the first word of a flesh-language
We always knew but only now have tasted
In the strong original: *Morr, Morr, Morsilka*.

War and Soup

(i.m. Georgi Valentinovich Drobyshev, 1907-1995)

Rear-Admiral (retired)
Of the Soviet Fleet,
Your father, wearing
His soiled cook's
Babushkin halad,
Manhandles down
From its several hooks,
The ticklish weight
Of the Samurai sword.
Losing no face
To the chopping-board,
It flashes before you
What it did in the old days,
And still might do
If it weren't a ploughshare.

In a distant kitchen
Forty years later,
You recall the scare.
Sand-speckled mortars
Rear up for food
As we watch the slow fade
From suits to bellicose
Huddles of khaki.
There was a peace-plan:
'Our hopes are high'...
Now I want to cry
Oh, let me see
That old sleight-of-hand –
Catastrophe twirled
To the windfall or wedding
Where good stories end!
But the telly glows
And roars. War wins.

The Samurai Chef
Keeps humming a tune
In your home-grown *skazka*.
He shifts a serene
And fabulous grip
As the sword makes deft
Green lacework of each
Noble napper.
Then he gathers the threads,
Lets them whirl and skip
In his own fairy-tale.
When the rumour is rich
Enough, he'll announce
The feast, and share,
Golden, unbloodied,
His bequest of soup-moons.

Even now, our spoons
Could kiss the breathing bowl.

Antrim Road Dream-House

The house hangs in the balance of our pockets,
As near, as far, as a remedy for cancer
Or love-in-absence, when we climb its core
To open rooms like gifts you rarely find
In January. A wing of summery light
Sheers up the highest wall, sinks to the raw
Wood of the staircase like a contract signed
In sky, a god's impulsive, longed-for answer.
Room, it says: room to repair homes broken
In haste, to be together and yet spacious,
Hospitable... The frame jolts forwards, then.
A wailing car warns us not to forget
What quality of mercy holds the keys
Of all this luxury, suspense, regret.

A Small Incendiary Device on Eglantine Avenue

After the bang, seven globes flowered softly
On their seven stems, curving
Tall above the roofs and the long street.
Hot grain ran down the night in fading tracks
And a stick with which some child
Had touched the sky, fluttered,
Star-burned, to our feet.

University Square Glue Grove

You are not fooled, as the young are often fooled,
By local sound effects, light-shows in the sky.
You'd never trust a tomorrow you couldn't buy
And clutch, close as a lover's face, as food,
Today. It looks like honey, it looks warm.
You chase it with an earful of some beat
Safe as bad news, the eternal bytes that swarm
Round blunt machines for making human meat,
And wave to say that everything's dead-on
From up there in your personal pleasure-dome.
Elsewhere, God's air is smoking round a ton
Of slithering bricks, but this is Sweet Life Street,
The customs tightly zipped as 'formal' dresses.
Our chestnut empires, steeply, aptly, fallen
Though they appear, aren't metaphors – just guesses.

The Disentitlement

The name peels off: it was never mine.
And the face – a scaredy child's,
Stealing because it was told to.
Take it, where time goes down without a fight–
History. The night I made it,
My smithereen cobweb with the coal-black spider
Screamed, but I screamed louder:
Don't think you know what it's like,
You cushy bastard, till you've been out here
In the freeze-frame, knowing for sure
Your day had come and now it never would.

Eyes

Reflectionless, opaque,
The "pig" slips by, unmanned
Apparently, no Janus faces turned
By monstrous separateness.

City of torn eyes,
How many can command
A single gaze?
How many does it take?

About the Jews

(from the Russian of Boris Slutsky)

Jews don't plant wheat.
Jews trade in corner-shops.
Jews go bald earlier.
More Jews are thieves than cops.

Jews are adventurers,
No good at war.
Ivan fights in the trenches.
Abram minds the store.

I've heard it since my childhood
And soon I'll be decrepit.
Still I can't escape it:
The chant of 'Jews, Jews'.

I've never been in trade.
I've never stolen, once.
I carry this damned race
Inside like a disease.

The bullets didn't get me
Which only goes to prove
None of the Jews was shot.
They all came back alive.

Transfusion

How can you learn to treasure what you have?
Not by watching the wing of day's no-colour
Smearily born from dawn's attempt at blue
Like a ghost's ghost-child. Not by trying to count
All those closed eyes that might have cupped with love
The coldest light. Not by telling your story
In a different voice, because it might have been
A different story, had you not guessed too late.
This breath you gather daily to regret
All your cast bread, which rots, contemptuous
As a road-block on the one road you must take,
Will be treasure only if so deeply given,
That, on some border, miles, or a mile, away,
Feathers of air begin quivering, in pulse-time,
The shirt-front of a child, who may lie stiffly,
But seems, all the same, to point to the future
In an eager, jerky line, from soles to scalp.

The Stowaway

Shiver of air
In a mean angle of my sliding door,

My hand, a cup
That dances with you, tries to catch you up,

How many hits
And misses till you're crushed, your wings in bits?

Last night, the friend
Driving me home talked politics without end.

I got so dull,
Spooled in the thick of the theoretical;

I wanted grief
Even for the smeared fur, glazed disbelief

That cried in front of us:
Gods of the hedgerows, hell is also this!

This morning, you
Are the only nightmare I can make untrue:

Two lace-snippets, brown,
With one pink thread in each, to tease a bald pink clown,

A monster, blind
And heavy, not unkind, but not your kind,

Stunned by her own
Haphazard wits, admonished when you turn

Your shy skull-face
And trust a finger for your perching-place.

You pause, intent
On measuring with some secret instrument

Where on earth you are,
Relative to the moon or some moth-star.

What's in the mind
You wear outside your delicate head? The wind

May know, not I.
Has autumn touched your pulse, said *time to die?*

You won't find rest
In this back yard. A beech-wood suits you best,

Not human sighing:
Have roads and rooms destroyed your mood for flying

Or is what slows
Your take-off just the cross-wind of bad news,

The stench and sirening where-
Ever a human breath enters the atmosphere?

The Border Builder

No soonor had one come down
   Than he began building again.
My bricks, O my genuine bricks
   Made of my genuine blood!
What would we be without borders?
   So which one are you? he said
And stuck out his hand to me.
   Birth certificate? Passport?
Which side are you on, which side?
   Merrily he unrolled
Starry dendrons of wire
   To give his wall ears and eyes.
Qualifications? he said.
   Residence permit? Tattoo?
Which colour are you, which colour?
   No colour, he said, no good.
He took my only passport,
   He slammed it down on the wire.
My hand, O my genuine hand!
   This is a border, he said.
A border likes blood. Which side's
   Your bloody hand on, which side?

Variations on a Theme of July

I said *Where am I?*, thinking love said *Home*.
Instead, the light remarked on absent eyes.
Quicker, then, than midsummer could revise
Its plans, clouds take apart their moonstone houses,
A ship of iridescences went down
In slights and tears and lies.
The light is matt and noisy, now, marched flat.
Ridiculous flags stick out of windows. Lies.
(My native land could tell you just what size.)
They close in shock, the rock-scarred irises
Of never-golden hills, the blanching skies.
Where do they meet, these blues, this greenishness,
And mix the colour, *home*? Is *home* more lies?
This valley is a confluence of lies,
A conference of doubling, turning faces.
They tried to be true colours, but kept shifting
Climate, slewed by something that could kill,
Pretending kindness, suddenly unpretending.
I know these Sunday paramilitaries
Who build in stone inside a child, make grey
Warships that can't be lifted
By love nor sea. But what is lost, can't find
A name and cannot tell its colour, cries
In me, touching the nerve of a like mind.
Poisoner, realist, filterer, fantasist,
I bed and breathe, dress and re-dress the lies,
Homely as rain, all-coloured as young eyes.

A Cloud House

(to 'the loneliest person who ever lived')

You loved the houses mist builds on a bay
As well as smaller shells on scurrying flits
('Compression, lightness and agility,
All rare in this loose world'), and casually
Forsaken homes of lapsed, unkillable arts
To do with fish. There's not much sea this way,
But, once, an Irish poet found amethyst
And moonstone in his air: you'd glimpse them, too,
And like the watery naming of these streets –
Moonstone, Capstone, Larkstone – as I do.

This well-worked stone is North – another reason
You'd quickly feel at home, as guest, as ghost,
Pleased by the manner, more pleased to discern
A climate amiable, reserved, unfussed
And modern. Since that summer night when rooms
Swam to the stars in Belvoir and our streets,
Privileged, stunned, got thick with speculation,
We've not – touch wood – heard much bad news. Our panes
Are loosened more by DIY, or trains –
Blue-streak expresses, shambling ochre freights.

Come to the window. We have clouds again,
Opal and pearl, with slate-blue undersides,
Clear harebell light, after a week of rain.
Small hills are tucked beyond the railway-line:
This seepage is the evidence of their trades.
The hills are shy, but the clouds are like your Moose,
Looming, curious. They'd have tea with us,
And mope and float their way through every room,
Dowsing the puzzled cactus, spelling doom
To the carpets, where they'd roll like exiled seas.

We'll shut them out. Instead, here's your *Complete
Poems*, the bookmark at 'Insomnia' –
That slender glass of sorrows, almost neat
But for the salt which makes great art's *tequila* –

Speaking of which, we'll share a drop some night
– Not yet. We know, as puritans, that we are
The natural victims of the iridescent,
The bright slide, hard to quit, once started on.
Your poetry is the finer consolation:
If it can't cure the poet, it charms the peasant.

Dusk's glow gets blue-er. Midges mob the door:
They tangle sideways, whizz like particles
In a cloud-chamber, dance like demented stars.
Are they in love? Is it sex they're celebrating,
Or some dank river-god under my floor?
This, it appears, is a midge's time of year,
Or else it's you that set them off competing,
Frantic to win a moment of that gaze
Which mapped the world so beautifully to scale,
From peak to shack to hummingbird-tiny detail.

Is fixity the gist of what I'm saying,
Or, at a wilder guess, posterity?
Although compared with you, I'm only playing
At exile, I'm disturbed by fixity,
Yet wish there were no choice but to be fixed.
This house remembers (something in it does)
How, back before the plumbing climbed the stairs,
Eight lives (six small, two slightly bigger) mixed
In a quartet of beds where one now sits.
They would have been contemporaries of yours.

The latest I could picture on these streets,
Goes to church twice a week, loves Twelfth parades.
She sometimes still gets sent communion-cards,
So, named, survives this era of short-lets
To foreigners like me. If, one cold night,
Anne Walker should come back, drawn by my light,
Who'd be the ghost? Whose would be the home?
And what am I to you, fumbling about
The sealed, transparent window of a poem?
No love can let me in, nor let you out.

The sky puts on her drabbest violet now;
The moon sighs at her sixteen-hour day.
But none of this can matter where you are,
Out in space-time. You have forgotten how
Your gift was weighed in unwept tears of stone,
And how your houses liked to disappear
Into the radiant bays. Our spinning ocean
Cannot rest yet but you, I think, may stay
Becalmed at dawn. The stars burn gently there.
And you are shadowless, and far, and dear.

CELTIC MYTHS

Two Windowscapes
(for Jean Bleakney)

I

I watched a pulse of rainbow as it faded,
A sky-traced heart-beat, strong at first, but failing
And lost before my light-enchanted cones
Could mix the waves, my mind still lost for labels.
A rainbow's something else than seven plain tones.
It's less like paint than pastel, hazy, shy
With inbetween shades, namelessly embraided.
That's why it seems so human and so tender.
A rainbow surely views us through the eye
Through which it's viewed – the cataracts, the floaters,
The dazzle and the weather-scattered panes.

II

The sky was milk, plum-frozen to the bottle.
Suddenly, it had drained. The light went dead.
Something was slowly puzzling out the world,
Groping along strange air-ways, lost, and then
Boldly it took possession. Like a playground
My window teemed, all moving, all enchanted.

Original human sin – to be enchanted!
To see a freckled girl emerging where
The laurel glowered – north her safe house, Apollo
Slack in Ash Wednesday shrouds – to say it's hope
Or faith, at least, in the wingbeat of that sparrow
Who skims the yard wall, shivers so strongly up
Through the caves and pantries of cotoneaster,
It seems she's got a site marked out, already
Becoming fact among the water-nests
The snow keeps fixing and dissolving there.

The First Storytellers

They said there was a house, and something in it
Formed by the satin-finish light would give
An indoor-courtyard, by the dusky sift
Of irons welcoming fire, and duckdown, sleep.
There was a rind as well, where pigeons shuffled
And shook their iris ruffs, and lived aslant,
Happy as slates, as clouds in a cloudy heap.
Some say that Time had found a place to live,
But Earth would not move in, so no one did,
Though there was flesh, and blood, and voice, and feeling,
As the first frightened witnesses declared,
A hand in water, a shadow on the ceiling,
Senses that knew light died each day, and grieved
And invented a demon to be tender with.

True North

Here, every man claims to have a brother.
The women say nothing.
Men kiss each other's faces with their fists
Till womanish blood flows.
The ladies know that's foolish.
They put a cheek to a cheek to keep it cold.
Here, scholars agree
'Cunt' is a generic noun,
So how can a poet possess one?
Here, women use themselves
As scissors, files, dividers, compasses.
They make out they're not murdering each other.

The Close Reader

Calmly and very carefully, like a thief
Of the old school, silk-fingered in the drawer
He'll leave not quite just-so in the master bedroom,
I check each word until a troubling, low
Vibration earths it, and the author's voice
Sing-songs, harsh and playful, from the drive.
I go on searching, even as I hear
The lighter footsteps, innocent on the stairs.
Face meets astounded face. But nothing shatters...
I move back to the drawer. Carefully, calmly,
I turn the jewels to light them with reflections:
The husband-soiled, husband-enchanted lips,
The sometimes eager, sometimes clouded, eyes.

Cycle

The blush-winged smile of Arianrhod the Swift,
Burned hard as copier-light, giving eyes to memory.
Each curtsey of kitchen-houses offered a hill,
Mottled with rose or rust, from her apron pocket.
And the road was becoming a tree
Of left-handed sentences, reaching
And over-reaching, until
Alexandria. Clouds were the only war,
Till the birth of love cried out in mortal language.
The flung wheels, ludicrous,
Raced on their sides and, in self-punishment,
Slashed to ringlets she child's forgetful fingers.

The Safest Grazing

The faults in your secret, most unwashable linen:
A dot of iron-mould, a thread of hair,
The crumpled proof love packed you without care;
A wax seal, shiny with old needle-pain:

Is there no dusk so kind you'd release its hills
To these small scapegoats, roam with them to where
A thirst might lose itself in thirsty ripples,
And blushes close both eyes, or sly and lively,
Notice the look that declares their causes lovely?

Peat Fire

I broke into archaeology, uncorked
Death-champagne, gold fizz for the black throat,
But all that's left in my small-hours hearth is flaked
Skin from her rough heels, and her tattered sandals.

Morning Card

A space between words, in which no word will fit.
Colour's decay. A fifties TV,
Abandoning its hold on the vertical.
Sentences needling through the mind at heart-rate,
Muttering furiously: *we can explain.*
A window, white and insatiable as a letter
With an unslept blackness round it.
Notification of a day, a funeral.

Self-Portrait from a Prison

Rain thickens to scent and this is leaf-memory, its quick decay loading the sky with pewtery, antique brain-clouds.
If those are daisies, outliving the newly-clipped grass that smells of *zubrovka*, their eyes are all fingers, pleading
For bed-time, like sick children. The horse-chestnuts have flung down their tapers, refuse to unshadow their precious caves.
It is not even hope that vanished with the rain, but the scald of hope lost. The leaves all point to one future – the foot-patrol.
And a little girl is hooked sharply under the chin, made to tilt up her frown. Once, thank God, I'd seen the last of her shyness:
Now she's back inside, the child who found her false smile, her lost tongue, her wet blanket on every glint and ambiguity,
Who was after all irreversibly turned to stone.

War of the Tongues

(a mock epic)

I

When I first heard her voice with its under-swell
Of a child's gruff lullaby to itself,
My heart undid like an old-fashioned pillow.
I could no longer speak
My language as she is spoke in the fatherland.
Rhotic abeyances, spurned vowels,
The stammerer's curse against the silencer,
Were charmed into surely ever-renewable
Volumes from her wood-sweet Linen Hall,
Our names twinned and carved in their secret spines.

One affricative could have held me
Like a sea never meeting, always surpassing
The lip of the shore, like a Russian abstract noun
Wiping the ache from its forehead with a soft-sign.
Slagged off, my boat would have danced
On its curly-leaved ancestors,
And havened safe in any wind of Antrim.

II

Instead, her courtesies proved me the enemy.
The keel of my tongue was split,
Rock battered the brow of that S.P.A.D.E.
In the land she gave me with one hand, took with the other,
True son of my cut-throat heart.

I draw on this, my last imperial art –
The shutting up of poets.
But the leaves I kill at night are clay tomorrow
In my cold engine room, still readable,
Making me doubt what happens
To human texts when they are deconstructed
Even in the fiercest temperatures.

And I draw on myself but it's sketchy,
A few red crossings-out while tuning in
To the choppy waves between
Two-Way Family Favourites and *Fáilte Isteach*,
And the bath-taps whistle me home.

Sip me, foam, whisper your nothings, truer
Than any west of hers, much less a
Bare-faced lie than mine.

Song of the Non-Existent

This is the hour between dog and wolf, when the first
Anxiety walks across to the polished counter,
And the sky becomes lighter and darker at the same time,
And the moon, if it shows, is a pale, inessential detail

Because this is the hour of glass, the age of souls;
Gold is in every leaf, and to walk in the glow
Between traceries is to be among the angels:
This is the page on which you write the word 'angels'

And the muse, though stern, doesn't flinch: when impotent wings
Of learning stretch to the cloudiest stony hill:
This is the net of desire, where something adrift and homeless
Is caught and pronounces itself a nightingale.

This is the wolf's hour, after all; he turns it between his teeth:
The watery city thickens, blackens: all that the angels leave
Is this: your sudden reluctance to remember
How hard it was, and how beautiful, to live.

To the Spirit of My House

By the fire for the last time in Maryville Avenue,
Will I sit watching your hair unscroll in the flame?
Your hair's not red, not a mass of flowing curl,
Though perhaps it was, when you were a little girl:
Nevertheless, you brought to my hearth one night
Your paler colours, flowing to fill your name,
And, as you left, the coals seemed sunk in regret.
The fire has known ever since how to conjure you.

And when I eat my last meal at the book-strewn table,
Carelessly heaping rice from the foil tray,
Will I glance up and find you opposite me,
A guest, reduced to fast food by an unplanned visit?
Will one of us remark – 'Not too bad, is it,
Considering it's the local take-away?' –
And, smiling, suggest we make the informal a habit –
Two women who rarely cook, and never feel noble.

And when I go to my last sleep under this roof-space,
Will I think how a miracle just might have occurred,
Though miracles don't exist in any world
I've ever lived in, and find you casually pressed
To me, no edge, no softness, uncaressed?
Dazed with belief and disbelief, shall I stroke
Your crisp, un-flame-like hair, shall I lie awake
To study the miracle of a sleeping face?

And when I've shrunk it to boxes, this life I had,
Will I slam the door for the last time, locking you in
Firmly, leaving you ample time for despair,
While the orchard screams, and the dryads rend their clothing?
Will you tremble slowly to dust, and then to air?
Will I at last be alone, moving freely, breathing –
Or, as I turn the new key, sense something familiar
And wounding there, and be idiotically glad?

Math, Remembering

From long-stemmed words with their tender, watery perfumes,
I, no god, somehow created a woman.
For the first time, magic was simple.
I wondered: had I not known this all along?

But my flowers were only roots, sticky with soil,
Screaming in ugly voices – *we are not yours.*
Stems became bony, petals sharpened and fledged
And drew on my skin with long, scarlet claws.

To Blodeuwedd, Flying

Though hidden from me now, you're changing as if
The weathers of my heart still poured across your face,
And my hand-made sighs kept rearranging you.
What use are the winds of absence, strong and scentless,
When you constantly swing round like the month of April,
Flaunting different petals, letting me touch you
More artfully and hopelessly than ever
For having let you loose from earthly keeping.

Flauer-Mush

Cradle-snatched, done up like a dog's dinner,
   Leaves, buds, stalks an all
     Shoved in the kisser
Of some Lord Muck I never clapped eyes on before,
That can't tell a buncha dandelions from a gorse-bush,

I'm soon browned off being is precious Flauer-Mush,
   Trimming me cu'icles, touching up me roots,
Balancing bloody great jew-drops on me eyeballs,
   And going around in a fog
And sniffing meself and forever squirting me doodahs.

So when Miss P.-the-Bed-Buttonole (yours truly)
   Feels Muvver Erf comming on strong,
   And, *Duckie*, she says wivver eyes, *Go daun on me*,
     I says to is Lorship, *So long!*
     And I take the weight off me feet.

I'm *the flower of the oak and the broom and the meadow-sweet*
   Till it seems I got old of the wrong end of the stick
     And I'm sweet Fanny Adams. Chucked.
   Blow me! I could've swore she was lapping me up.
   So now I'm – excuse me French, like – fucked.

She pulls me ribs aut, snaps em in two, makes wings.
   Get lost, she says. I don't need asking twice.
     I'm staggering up into space,
     Screaming blue murder, shitting
White, dropping bits an bobs from me brain an fings.

Now the cockeyed buggers've got me where they always wanted.
   I'm mangey an gory an queer,
   Old Flauer-Mush, off me rocker, outa me tree
And a bird into the bargain – well – I ask you –
   A bleedin owl – a bloomin old softie like me!

Tír Fá Tonn

I was plunged in your dampest mood, my face had pearled over
Like the skin of an aeroplane suddenly scarfed by cloud.
A second higher, I found your shining mirror.
Rose-petals stained us, as if we had swallowed too quickly
   Too much new wine, and we were a compact, opened
Shyly as Venus's shell. Well, that day's skin is all dust now.
We've rendered to Cloacina, who weaves the world,
The gifts that are hers, and the troubled streams of those fingers
   I stilled without touch, have become the geologist's nightmare –
A rock-formation unique to vanished islands.

Iris and the Hailstone

None of the weather-stirring hills predicted
She'd pick the stone up, turn it idly round.
She was dressed in maps, and yet she'd never read
Of rainbows being started in a hand.

Unnoticed, unforeseen, the stone thinned
To a bleb of dew, like Odras when she fell
As a little startled rain at Morrigan's yell.
This time, too, there was a cry to estrange
Matter from its laws: then a great arm
Of rainbow stemming from a seared palm,
A rainbow stemmed, a stone tossed out of range.

Best China Sky

A primrose crane, a slope of ochre stacks,
Stencilled on tissue-thin
Blue, and, flung between
These worlds, a sword-flash rainbow,
The cloud it lies against,
Metallic as its topmost skin,
And, round the eyes of hills,
Tha tender bluish-green
That quickly yellows.

The prism comes and goes:
Wonderful stain, transparency of art!
A smoke-wraith sails right through it.
But now it strengthens, glows and braves its span,
You'd think it was the rim
Of some resplendent turquoise plate,
Offering hills and cranes and streets and us
Fancies designed to melt
As our fingers touched them.

Prayer for Belfast

Night, be starry-sensed for her,
Your bitter frost be fleece to her.
Comb the vale, slow mist, for her.
Lough, be a muscle, tensed for her.

And coals, the only fire in her,
And rain, the only news of her.
Small hills, keep sisters' eyes on her.
Be reticent, desire for her.

Go, stories, leave the breath in her,
The last word to be said by her,
And leave no heart for dead in her.
Steer this ship of dread from her.

No husband lift a hand to her,
No daughter shut the blind on her.
May sails be sewn, seeds grown, for her.
May every kiss be kind to her.

LEARNING TO BE MORTAL

Riddle

Moving and still
I try to fill
The space I had –
An inch of hair,
Erect with fear,
The rest, melted.

Portent

Over patches of bloom that might be frost, or where frost lately died,
The little bird runs like a rumour, dark as the road, with a
    snow-streaked side.

Lament

You'll die, and never again will my lips have touched you,
Your living mouth, nor my sleep have known such stillness.
Like a slow wave, phosphorescent, your voice will have risen,
Will have fallen, too far off to have left my thoughts shining.
Never again, from your vivid, familiar cursive,
Will my name have leapt, like a loved child, into my arms,
So that I silently tell you: though *love* means anything, nothing,
In your hand it's my life. Nor will I wake as your birthday
Dawns on my powers of blessing, desires all the colours
Most true to your faithless iris. And still that day
Will come back and tear wound after wound in the calendar,
But you will have died. Or I'll have. What's the difference
    In the eternal absence of all cherishings?

Sickbed

I would have washed flowers for you.
I would have washed water for you.
I would have fed you sunlight from the bowl.
Too neat. Too simple. You were already ill
From the words I couldn't wash, their being true.

Literacy

Only once, not asleep, I met you.
   A book gazed into your face.
   Your woolly chrysalis hung
   At your side, untrembling as
      Your 'heaviest of flowers'.

When you sensed I was near, and looked up,
   Your eyes were between-coloured
   From the world of names. Your smile.
   Sightlessly kind, and your blush
      Belonged there, not to me.

Only once, not dreaming, I found you,
   So still, I could have touched you.
   If I were that book, I thought,
   That fingered, lingering page,
      Not this human nothing...

Circle

Suppose God only imagined Lucifer's slight
But, locked in a mask of injury, so revised him,
He, God-adoring, fell from the perfect dawn
That fleshed and winged him, into perfect night.
Suppose you are Lucifer, who were thus rewarded,
And suddenly the night is a dawn of flame.
They'll say you hurled the torches out of vengeance,
But you, confused, half-shining, will repeat
That everything you burned you burned for light.

Months

1 *Months as Mirrors*

September's light falls so like May's,
    You could forget the year had moved
At its grave, water-burdened pace,
    From, not towards, the place it loved,

And, moving, stretches hope too thin
    To bear a moment's fantasy
Where dead leaves fill their hearts with green
    And flock home to a sun-caged tree.

2 *Months as Graves*

My last children tip forwards, as if for bunny-hops,
Big forehead moons to little shapeless knees.
They had just begun to tumble into nowhere,
Still wrapped in their nesting-silk, when something froze them,
And they die into this photograph I'm making
From a sealed box and a last thread of mucus.

Death of an Afternoon Woman

'Something is pushing them
To the sides of their own lives'
PHILIP LARKIN, 'Afternoons'

A hand, was it? Or something heavier,
Swooping with the down-swing,
Its shoes packed with meat
And little bones chipped from my own?
At first I didn't resist:
I'd be kicked anywhere,
Sit smiling on the farthest seat.
Was life mine to be lived?
Almost against my will,
As the chain-swings swooped, I heard
The seas divide.
I was walking a paper stillness,
A perfect centre parting
Through the roar of weather.
My life? Thanks. I'll rhyme it.
I'll keep it.
Keepers losers, they whispered
And I woke up.
If this is my house, it's mist,
If this is my land, water,
Constantly traversed
By miniature heels, child-hands,
Wide open, chainless.
The force I feared is so small,
I could catch it in a caress
And run with it to wherever
It tells me our home is.

Science Fiction

Once, you beat the midnight with new heels,
Spritzing the granite to stars
For happiness that it led to such small hours.
You hummed home taxi-less,
Disaster-proof with love or alcohol:
You could have been a bi-plane
Among the galaxies and their song-like legends:
Bawnmore. Grand Malone. Shy Maryville. Moonstone.

Spilt milk, now, unnavigable
Astrologies of chaos.
There are no meetings in this universe.
Lock up, stay put. If midnight brings some footfall
Quick to your door, a knock, a silence stretched
Until the silence cries,
Ask who would seize your lips,
Post-code, shoes: what mutant?
Don't turn the latch for her because she whispers
She was your happiness. Don't be taken in.

Like It Is

Leaf of the thistle   trickster of the immune-system
Truth of the vino   new mole in the tan
Stain on the shirt-front   training in the infant
Date on the Visa-card   virus of the scan
Slug in the lily   lily in the ploughed field
Hot blood of Blodeuwedd   owl of her *hiraeth*
Burn of the X-ray   politeness of the official
Story of your life   one-liner of your death

Christmas Letter from the Boss

Dear World,
        I notice the butcher's dressing the tree
Again this year, which is just as it ought to be:
I love a nice traditional ceremony.
You know the shortest root to Eternity?
Yes, martyrdom. Don't take life personally.
You've got to die, so why not die for me?
A cross or a bomb, a smile blown off, or a knee –
And you'll soon be doing lunch in my carvery.
Give my regards to Salman. Tell him he
Fits the author-shaped space in my ego. Hopefully
He'll be up soon for a salver of kedgeree.
I'll sign off now, and, remember, death makes you free.
Keep up the struggle, lads.

                    Yours,
                    I. D. Ology

The Loneliness of the Vertebrates

The slope of your back as it rises, flows over your shoulder,
    Never fails, as you pass, to shock me with tenderness.
You are sixteen, twenty, at most. You'll never grow older
    Than your lonely, upright back – nor I, turning mine, grieve less.

The Hag of Beare in Limerick

Suddenly, most of me's useless,
My cunt, unattended and juiceless,
    My tits, never sucked,
    My thermostat, fucked,
And my brain, like old Newsletters, newsless.

The Amateur Electrician

Engineers make good lovers, they know how the body works
And with tender skill arrange small tributes and pleasures.
I'm no engineer, but I understand low forms of practical magic.
I'd give you a city Christmas, fountains of colour, lacings of wind-
    shivered brilliance,
If you would trust me to be your electrician.
But if you just wanted to sleep undisturbed in your deep country
    nightfall
Of fading rush-light and stars, that would be fine with me, too.

The Terms

Only as if you had been a child,
Even in my dream and my lament.
Inviolable. Held
Only if whole, fierce, single. Only lent.

From a Conversation During Divorce

It's cold, you say, the house.
Yes, of course I'll go back one day,
Visit, that is. But the house

Will be cold, just as you say.
Two people have left home,
One of them me, and one

Our youngest child. So of course
It's cold, just as you say,
And big, too, bigger at least

Than it was with everyone there.
Don't think I don't think about you
Being cold in a house that size,

A house that gets bigger, too,
And colder each time I dare
Think about you and the house.

It used to be warm in the days
Before I decided to go,
And it didn't seem big at all,

In fact, it was rather small,
Which is partly the reason I...
Don't keep on asking me why

And telling me how it is
In the house. I don't want to know.
How can I go back, how can I

Even visit a house that size,
And getting bigger each minute
With all the cold rooms in it?

Threnody for a Leader

The mother we were free to hate is dead.
The last we saw of her, her face was breaking:
Only the palace of her hair still stood.
Her sons threw off their sullenness and cheered.
Her daughters, too, denied their hearts were aching.
We knew she'd leave us nothing. She loved men,
Next to herself, and we were none of hers.
But, yes, we thought her of some consequence –
Stronger than us, because she'd had to be;
Stronger than men. This proves the fallacy.
Her triumph, like her wealth, was all men's making,
And now she's in their funny cupboard world,
Upside down, her voice a box of holes,
Blue sparklers jammed in the hollow of her head,
While they charge round the room with guns and shrieking,
And swear they'd rather die than play with dolls.

Here I Am

(from the Russian of Bella Akhmadulina)

Here I am at two in the afternoon,
Held up by the midwife like a trophy.
Lutes play over my head, fairy-wands
Tickle me. All my soul understands
Is a flood of golden colour; here I am
On a burning day the summer before the War,
Gazing around at the beautiful creation.
With lullabyes and Pushkin ('The Snowstorm'),
I get into the habit of being alive.
But here I am, ruined by war, alas,
Subject to Ufa's gloomy supervision.
Winter and hospital, how white they are!
I notice that I haven't died. Those called
Instead, are blurry faces in the clouds.
Here I am, brimming with eagerness,
Ugly, bluish, body just set free,
Alert to something tinier than a sound.
Not until later will I value this
Habit of hearing an eternal roll-call
Of nameless things in my name-giving soul.
Here I am, decked in purple, haughty,
Young and fat. But I have trained my mouth
To shape the smile of a poet before death.
There is a game between word and word
That's like the trembling between heart and heart.
The single obligation is to trace it
Flowingly, with a casual, careful art.
These words are bride and bridegroom. Here am I
Declaiming, chuckling like a village priest
Who prays the secret union will be blest.
That's why the good fairies scatter whispers
And laughter. I'm extraordinary, marked out
By my forehead, my singer's curving throat!
I love these marks of singularity.
My hand dashes off like a young hound
After her prey, bringing it to the ground.
Here I am. But my soul stops. I can't move.

I curse and cry. Let the page stay white!
Even though it was given me from above,
My task could not be honourably completed.
I bend my neck to the torment of a harness.
How others weave their words, I couldn't say.
I haven't got the nerve, the craftiness.
Leave me alone. A little person, twin
Of everyone alive, here I am
Dozing on the train, my nodding face
Homely against my bag. I've little fame,
Thank God, and no more fortune than my neighbour.
I'm with my weary fellow-citizens,
Flesh of their flesh. It's good. Last in the queue
That stretches endlessly from the cashier's
In shops, cinemas, stations, I'm the one
After the cheeky youth and the warm-shawled
Old woman, merging with them like a word
From my language and a word from theirs.

The Judas Magnificat

Under the hot, declarative May sky,
The gorse pulsed, its oils both dark and bright –
Flawed, unsorry, streaming, near-immortal
Life-stuff the oldest hills would not gainsay,
But answered with a flush, a soak of excitement,
The light, an enormous, fragile bell of memory
To which the bell-less churches silently
Bent their brows. And all the acts of grace
The townlands knew, in their deep neighbourliness,
Unveiled, rose up against their own refusal.

Take nothing which is not freely given:
I'd studied – hard enough to have lost stones –
This hungry text, but everything alive
That day seemed freely given, not to accept
Or show companionship, a kind of murder.
Sitting together in the bus to Belfast,
We strung words between sunsets, watched ourselves
Until, beyond the speeding shade, our difference
Floated, a tiny grass-blade to the sky.
I thought, with dread, how our blushing-time would pale
And sicken west. But the light lay back, its smile
Deepened, if anything, as the traffic slowed us.

It seemed, back then, one kiss could mend all woundings.
Surely her unoffended smile would seal
Our truce, her peace? And, as I turned for home,
These smaller hills, patchy as aprons, strewn
And warmed with use like Sunday-night kitchens,
Though never doused in gold, would seem consenting,
The soiled air indelibly rinsed through
With all she was: her fire and shine and sweetness.

Summer Time Begins
(for Joan Newmann)

In a surprise of light
My chimney props its shadow
On the house-front opposite,
And the shadow-stack lets flow
An upward skitter
Of dirty curls, unstable
As local crosswinds.
If smoke and shadow-smoke
Changed place, how could we tell?
And which sign to trust:
The hills' milky sheaves
Of blizzard, swept low
By the gale's cutter,
Or the slow-widening
Harebell dusk that says
Kind days will soon come
Newly relaxing through
Each loaf-small home,
No smoke, no shadow-fire
Riddling, deriding,
But all we dared hope for
Made tangible: a second
Chance, an extra hour?

The Stone Butterfly

(for Kelsey & Rebecca)

Slow days, as a life prepares
To leave, discarding all
But its lightest necessaries.
Once we followed it
Through vivid stories, woven with our own.
We called it *Mum* or *Gran*, intimately.
Now, tired of our familiarity,
The life shifts, moves on
To a part we can barely read,
A hard, mysterious page, on which we glimpse
A figure so unselfconscious,
It could well be the long-ago child,
Scolded early to bed in her flowered nightdress.
The V-neck straggles across
The bare, innocent breast-bone,
The face, a kind of violence
To the face we expected, almost
As the child's must have been –
Flung open in grief or fury.
Fixed, now, beyond soothing.

But these are appearances, partial
Views from where we sit,
Tangled in life, still, bound
By its tentative aesthetics.
The rich, layered protein bundle
Was meant to unfold, has always been unfolding.
When the molecules first talked and had ideas
That would be this particular person,
They allowed the heart a pause,
A moment's doubt for every great iamb,
And cells, already orphaned,
Were drifting from the untouched skin of the new.
The losses, heavier now,
May seem more soul-like:
A little blood that darkens
In the crook of the catheter,
Hunger, proprieties, the speakable words.

But this is her soul, too, this make-do-and-mend,
This Londoner's painful wit
That almost cheats each shortage
By a shrug, a *good riddance*,
And the sudden panic when
The black-out curtain slips.
Her hands fly into the night, then, signalling,
Lost and raw as fledglings tossed on a wind
To practise, until space
Becomes feathered, homelier.

That's when the slow day slows
Again, curves inwards.
We arrive again, and find
The curtains have closed ranks,
Broody as women in smocks
Waiting delayed appointments, the bare
Night-bulb burning as blue
As the dry blue dawn, and on other, less smooth pillows,
Eyes making out the grown-up shapes of day,
The dice swept back into the misty dream-cup.
She travels with quiet hands now,
And has taken only the smallest morning with her
For the sharp descent that cannot
Get easier.

But it does get easier:
The bundle almost peeled, only a little
Breath still saved in the lining,
To be spent in precise measures
Like childbed breath, but less,
Much less of it. And we must concentrate
On a new, exacter climb,
Feeling for toe-hold, stooping
Sometimes to pick up a keepsake,
Greedy now we know how small and cool
A hand becomes, a shell
Though we bind it, warm it, in our drowning fingers.

There will be harder things:
Keys that open wounds, rings to be counted,
Skins to be cast or worn.
Ghosts will leave dust or mist on the least expected
Surfaces: an envelope, which states
In familiar wobbly ovals
And swoops of cursive: *everything in order.*
And at once the bent white head and aching fingers
Will be an image I
Wipe off like tears, freeing
Something clear and achieved, its pride, its kindness:
The mind-thread glistening black
And alive as the veins on wings,
As if an envelope could be
That brilliant, weightless life she always wanted –
A butterfly. A manila butterfly.

For a time, we'll throw the dream-dice
And thoughts will flutter and play
Over a different horizon.
The world, we'll say, is sufficiently beyond us.
Rich postcards will arrive
From Eternity, a resort
Not yet built, but scripting its foundations
In super-matter, somewhere.
So we'll fly as far as we know
And come back sad, because gravity
Seems to own every airline,
And sit like children again
Being shown how to read
One more time, till slowly
Words become things, things become words, souls
And proteins pool their resources
And matter's highest kite –
Poetry, love, whatever –
Is tenderly reeled in through the dusk. Never mind.

Large-grained, each moment now
Widens, becomes a breath,
A sip of breath, brought
In a cup, by a machine,
But work for the whole feather-weight musculature,
The hand pulling from mine, a tiny pull,
As the lungs are forced to accept it
Again, again,
That punch of oxygen
Which starts the crying, rhymes the story on
And on, through chapters of plot
And counter-plot, into flashback
And metaphor, until wordless,
Hard-won, thread-like whispers are all that remains.

The day retreats a step.
The eyes close, choosing,
With sweet honesty,
To make it night. And still
An after-thought, an ellipsis,
The tongue in breath-space, trembling
As if it could offer us
A small 'and then'. And then
The forehead, huge and distant,
Suddenly whiter and, though quickly pressed
By lips, much farther away.

How can we say what happened? What we saw
Is all that can be said.
We can wish, of course, so fiercely
We nearly pray: that the body forgot to feel
How hard breath was, that the grace of all it had loved
Was received in every cell.
But for you and me, the end
Of the story is still guesswork,
And it's only my search for a not-unhappy full-stop
If I say how it seemed:
That something slipped very quietly
And unhesitatingly over

The edge of the day. It didn't
Flutter, fan itself up
To the lapis gates, the open halls of nectar
But fell like a stone, a fruit-stone, newly folded
To re-unfold, its contract with the earth
Binding as that of the sky-winged butterfly,
And death, no less than flight,
A natural miracle.

NOTES TO THE POEMS

A Short Life with Gratispool. *Gratispool* was the trade-name of a photographic processing company that operated a postal service during the 1950s.

1950. The original poem by Yevgeny Rein was one of a sequence printed in *Znamya* (July 1991) under the title 'Anti-Clockwise'. M.F. Frunze was one of the founders of the Red Army. G.K. Ordjonikidze was a high-ranking member of Stalin's Politbureau. Koba was Stalin's nickname, and Lake Ritsa, in the Caucasus, was the site of his dacha.

The Purr. Russian cats say *morr*, not *purr*.

War and Soup. *Babushkin halad* could be translated as Granny's gown, in this case, an ancient dressing-gown. *Skazka:* folk-tale.

About the Jews. Boris Slutsky (1919-1986) was a major poet of the Soviet generation. Many Russians know this poem without being aware that Slutsky wrote it. First published in Boris Filippov's *The Secret Soviet Muse* (Munich, 1961), it wasn't published in Russia until after the poet's death, in 1987. The poem is taken from Yurii Boldyrev's 1991 edition of Slutsky's *Collected Works in Three Volumes* (*Sobranie sochinenii v trekh tomakh*), I, p.165.

A Cloud House. Elizabeth Bishop told Robert Lowell: 'When you write my epitaph you must say I was the loneliest person who ever lived' (*One Art: The Selected Letters of Elizabeth Bishop*, edited by Robert Giroux, Chatto, 1994). The quotation in the first stanza is from 'The Strayed Crab' (*Complete Poems*, Farrar Straus & Giroux, 1969).

Cycle. *Arianrhod:* literally, Silver Wheel, a goddess in Welsh mythology.

Self-Portrait from a Prison. *Zubrovka:* vodka made from the aromatic herb bison-grass.

War of the Tongues. *Fáilte Isteach:* the name of an RTE Radio request programme, aimed particularly at the Irish emigrant population.

Math, Remembering. To Blodeuwedd. Flying. Flauer-Mush. Cycle. These poems draw on events and characters from the Mabinogion, but do not adhere closely to the original narratives. Various texts suggested strategies for some of these poems, especially Alan Garner's *The Owl Service*, which so brilliantly and faithfully casts the 'Blodeuwedd' story in modern dress. An uncollected paper by Nuala ní Dhomhnaill suggested how Blodeuwedd may be interpreted as an earthy, rooted figure rather than merely flowery and ethereal.

Tír Fá Tonn: in Irish myth, the Land under the Waves, the happy Otherworld.

Iris and the Hailstone. Morrigan was an Irish war goddess. A mortal woman, Odras, was changed into a pool of water by Morrigan after Odras let her bull service one of Morrigan's magic cows.

Like It Is. The pronunciation of Blodeuwedd should be anglicised with a hard D in reading this poem. *Hiraeth* means *grief.*

The Hag of Beare in Limerick. Probably a mythological character, the Hag is the speaker in the medieval Irish poem, *Aithbe Dan Cen Bes Moro.* There have been a number of English translations: the one I know is *Ebbing* by James Carny (*Medieval Irish Lyrics*, Dolmen, 1985).

Here I Am. Bella Akhmadulina (*b.* 1937) wrote this poem in 1968, presumably in response to government criticism and suppression of her work. Her collections of poetry include *String* (1962), *Music Lessons* (1969), *Snowstorm* (1977), *The Garden* (1987) and *Selected Poems* (1987). She has translated extensively from the Georgian. 'Here I Am' is dedicated it to E.Y. and V.M. Rossels. Ufa is an industrial town in the Urals.